Who I Am

An Inspirational Scripture Coloring Book for Girls

by Erica Basora

ISBN 978-1-953751-31-7

This Book Belongs To:

_____

Introduction

This coloring book is designed to inspire young girls and help them discover who they are in the eyes of God. Through creative coloring pages and scriptural affirmations, readers will gain a better understanding of their purpose as they reflect on scriptures and meditate on the amazing words of God.

King David speaks about who we are and how we were created in Psalm 139:13-14 which says; "For you created my inmost being; you knit me together in my mother's womb. I praise you because I am fearfully and wonderfully made; your works are wonderful, I know that full well." A reminder of our uniqueness and the special place we have in God's heart. He created each of us with a special purpose. We are loved and treasured by God,

Enjoy this coloring book and the bonus journaling pages as you explore who God says you are and discover all that He has planned for you!

-xoxo *Erica*

I Am Loved

"You are precious in my eyes, and honored, and I love you."
Isaiah 43:4

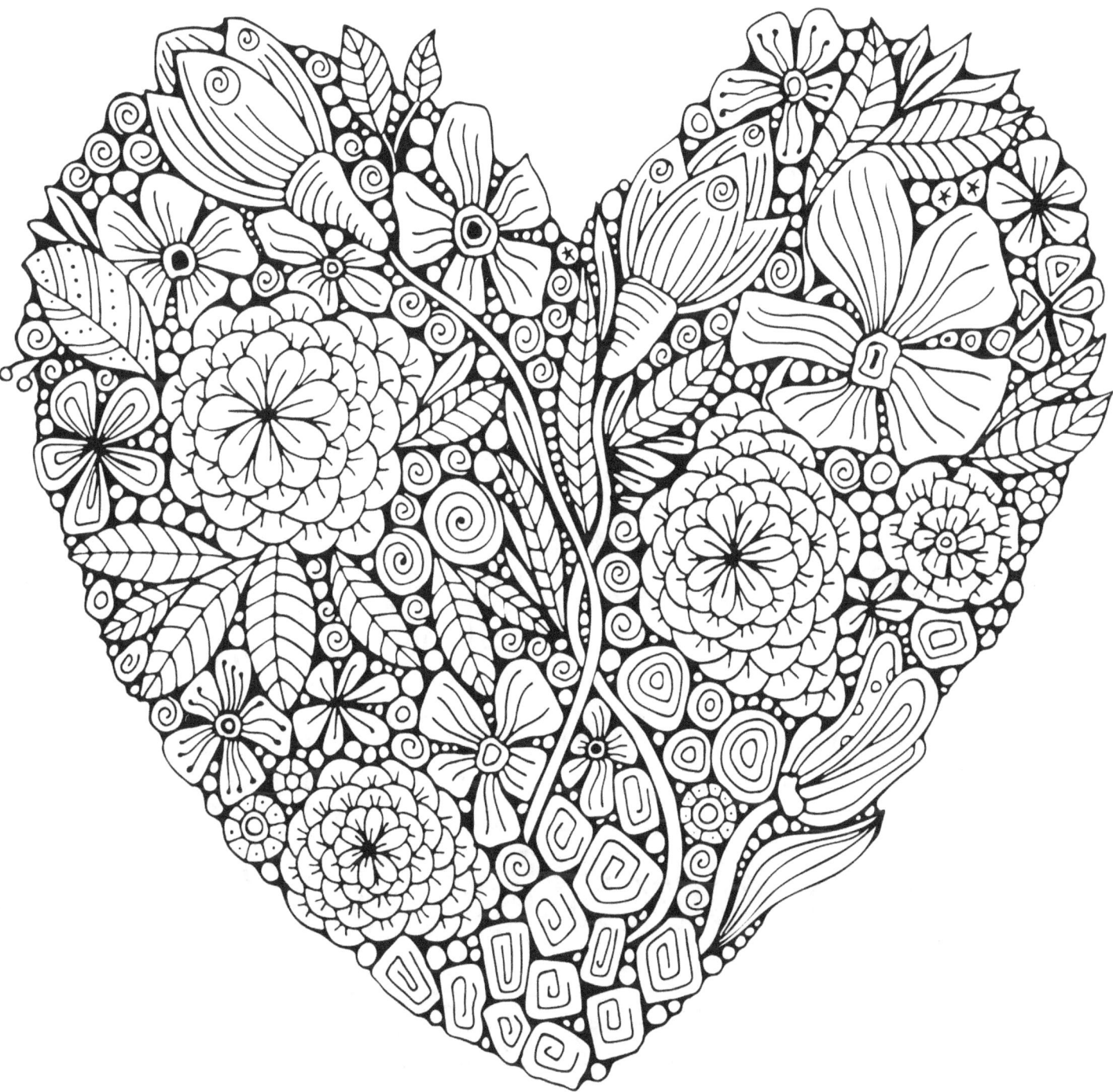

I AM
ANOINTED

♥ ♥ ♥ ♥ ♥

"You anoint my
head with oil; my
cup overflows."
Psalm 23:5

I AM
STRONG

"She is clothed with strength and dignity; she can laugh at the days to come."
Proverbs 31:25

I AM
WONDERFUL

♥ ♥ ♥ ♥ ♥

"I praise you, for I am fearfully and wonderfully made. Wonderful are your works; my soul knows it very well."
Psalm 139:14

I Can Do
All Things

♥ ♥ ♥ ♥ ♥

"I can do all things
through Him who
strengthens me."
Philippians 4:13

I AM THE SALT

♥ ♥ ♥ ♥ ♥

"You are the salt of
the earth;.. "
Matthew 5:13

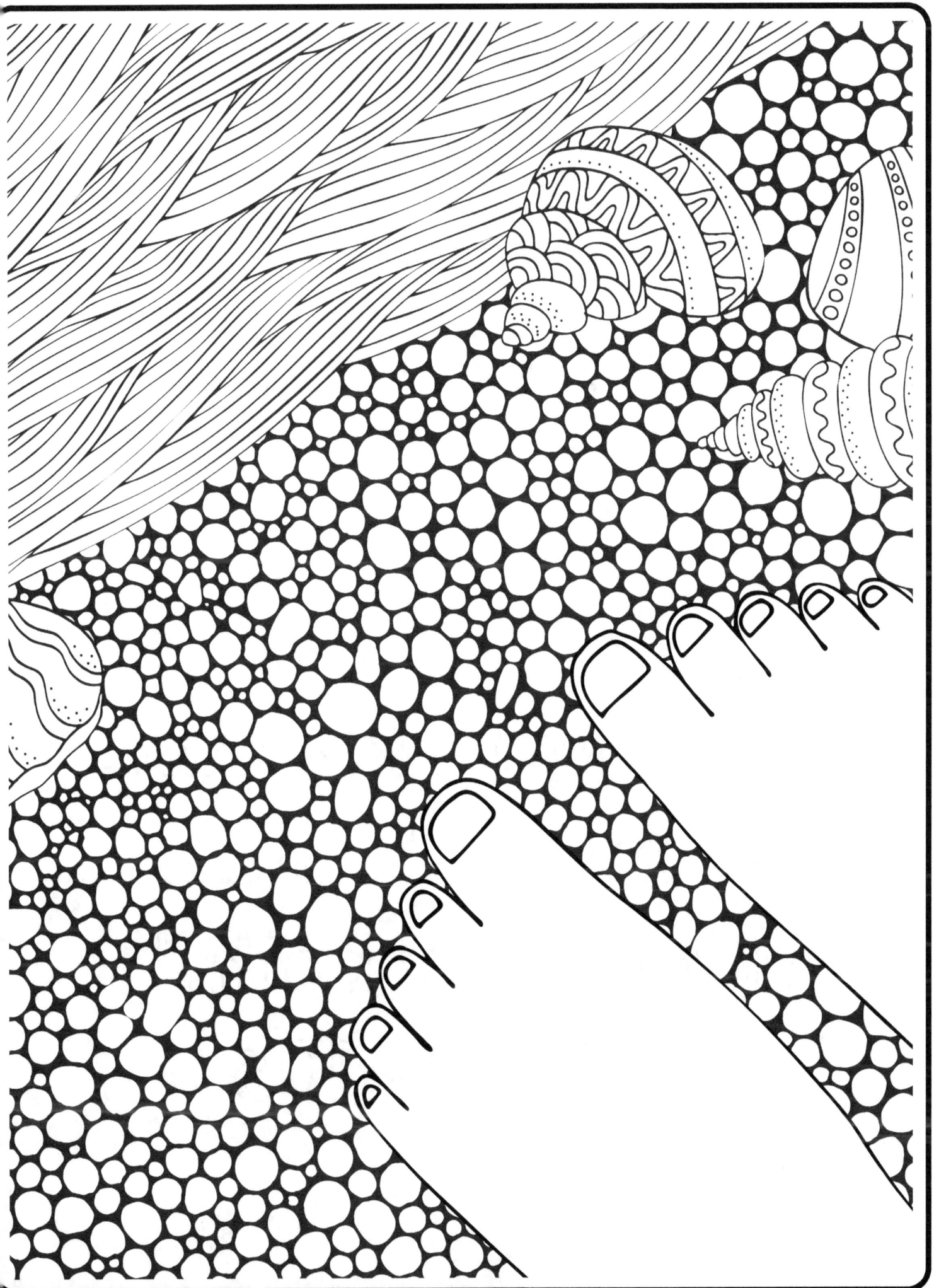

GOD'S WORD

♥ ♥ ♥ ♥ ♥

"Your word is a lamp to my feet, and a light to my path."
Psalm 119:105

I AM
ENOUGH

♥ ♥ ♥ ♥ ♥

"Your beauty should not come from outward adornment, such as elaborate hairstyles and the wearing of gold jewelry or fine clothes. Rather, it should be that of your inner self, the unfading beauty of a gentle and quiet spirit, which is of great worth in God's sight."
1 Peter 3:3-4

I AM
AT PEACE

♥ ♥ ♥ ♥ ♥

"The peace of God, which transcends all understanding, will guard your hearts and minds through Christ Jesus."
Philippians 4:7

I AM THANKFUL

♥ ♥ ♥ ♥ ♥

"Do not be anxious about anything, but in everything by prayer and supplication, with thanksgiving, let your requests be made known to God."
Philippians 4:6

I AM A CROWN OF GLORY

♥ ♥ ♥ ♥ ♥

"You shall be a crown of beauty in the hand of the Lord."
Isaiah 62:3

I DO NOT WORRY

♥ ♥ ♥ ♥ ♥

"And why do you worry about clothes? See how the flowers of the field grow. They do not labor or spin."

Matthew 6:28

I AM
TRUSTING

♥ ♥ ♥ ♥ ♥

"Trust in the Lord with all your heart.."
Proverbs 3:5

I AM A CHILD OF GOD

♥ ♥ ♥ ♥ ♥

"See what great love the Father has lavished on us, that we should be called children of God! And that is what we are!"
1 John 3:1

I AM GOD'S DAUGHTER

♥ ♥ ♥ ♥ ♥

"And I will be a Father to you, and you will be my sons and daughters, says the Lord Almighty."

2 Corinthians 6:18

I AM
HAPPY

♥ ♥ ♥ ♥ ♥

"Take delight in the LORD, and he will give you the desires of your heart."
Psalm 37:4

I AM THE LIGHT OF THE WORLD

♥ ♥ ♥ ♥ ♥

"You are the light of the world. A city that is set on a hill cannot be hidden."
Matthew 5:14

I HAVE A FUTURE

"For I know the plans I have for you," declares the Lord, "plans to prosper you and not to harm you, plans to give you hope and a future."
Jeremiah 29:11

I AM
FEARLESS

♥ ♥ ♥ ♥ ♥

"So do not fear, for I am with you; do not be dismayed, for I am your God. I will strengthen you and help you; I will uphold you with my righteous right hand."
Isaiah 41:10

I AM
COURAGEOUS

"Be strong and courageous. Do not be afraid or terrified because of them, for the Lord your God goes with you; he will never leave you nor forsake you."
Deuteronomy 31:6

I AM KIND

♥ ♥ ♥ ♥ ♥

"Therefore, as God's chosen people, holy and dearly loved, clothe yourselves with compassion, kindness, humility, gentleness and patience."
Colossians 3:12

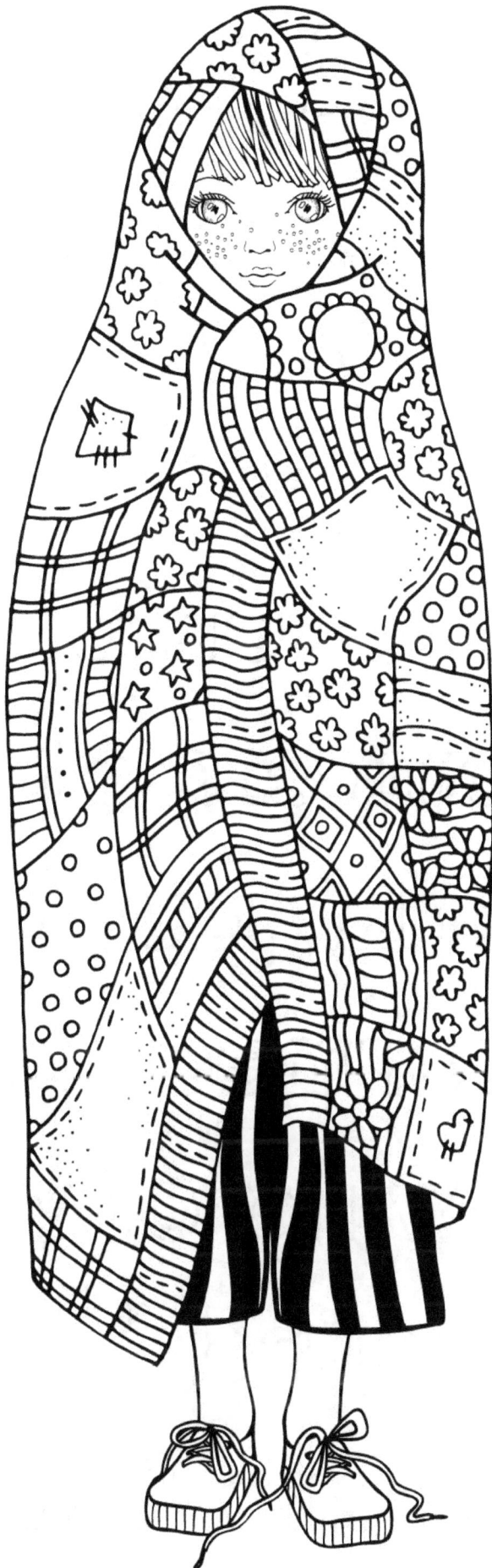

I AM
UNIQUE

♥ ♥ ♥ ♥ ♥

"Do not conform to the pattern of this world, but be transformed by the renewing of your mind."
Romans 12:2

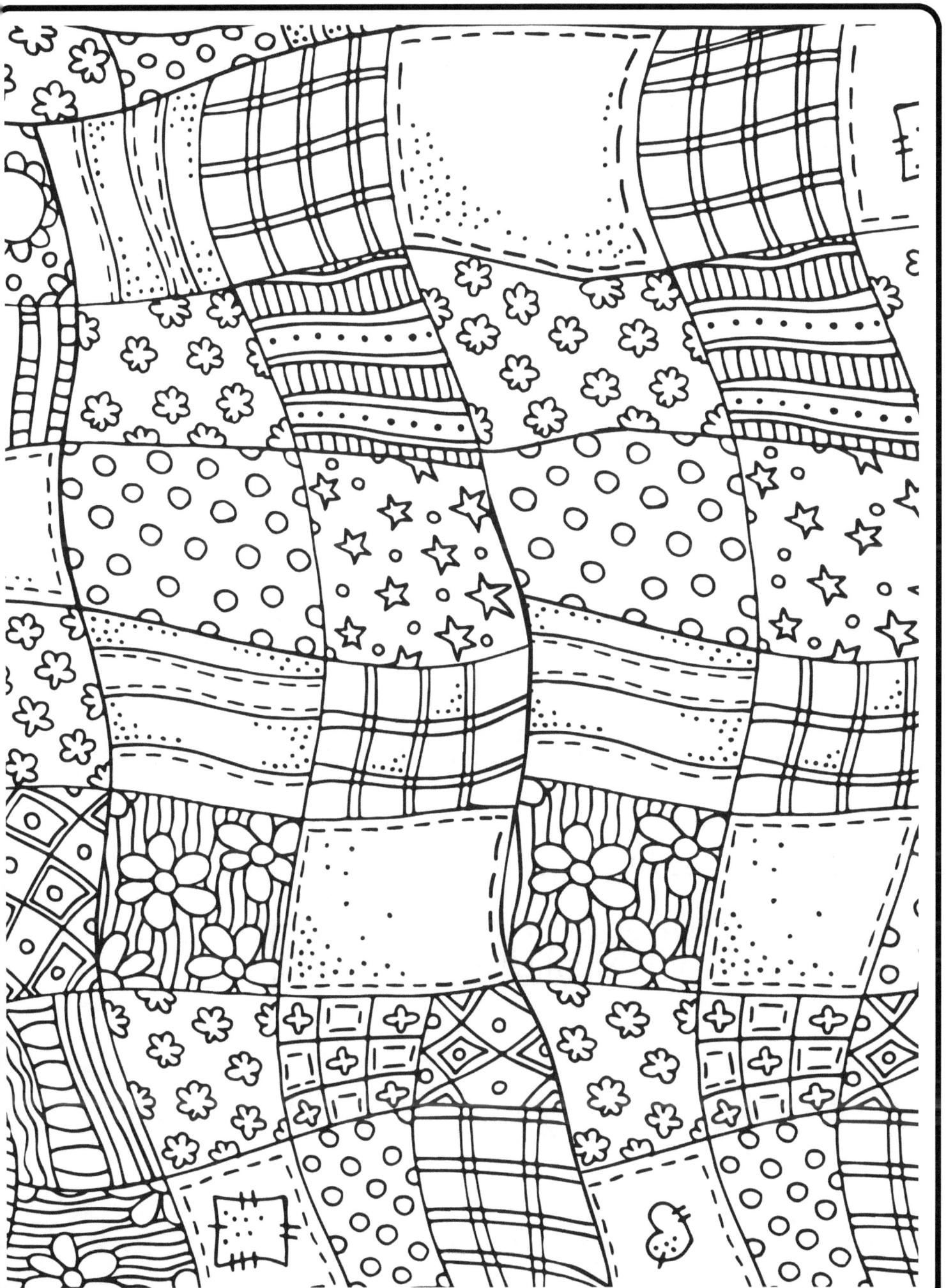

GOD MAKES MY PATH

♥ ♥ ♥ ♥ ♥

"You make known to me the path of life;"
Psalm 16:11

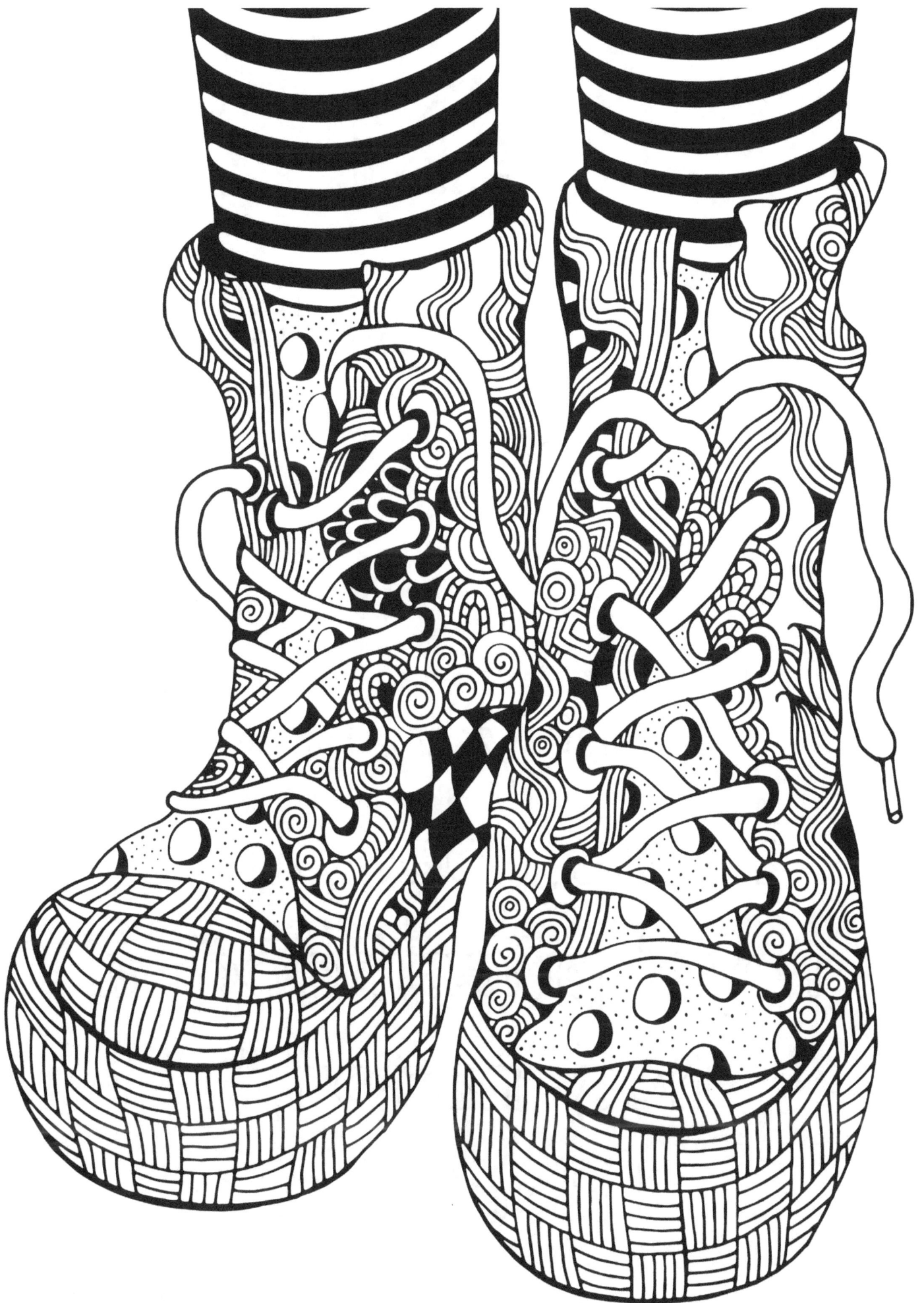

I AM CHOSEN

♥ ♥ ♥ ♥ ♥

"But you are a chosen people, a royal priesthood, a holy nation," 1 Peter 2:9

I AM
WISE

♥ ♥ ♥ ♥ ♥

"For wisdom is more precious than rubies, and nothing you desire can compare with her."
Proverbs 8:11

I AM
PRECIOUS

"She is more precious than rubies; nothing you desire can compare with her."
Proverbs 3:15

I AM
NOT ALONE

♥ ♥ ♥ ♥ ♥

"And surely I am with you always, to the very end of the age."
Matthew 28:20

I AM
WITH YOU

♥ ♥ ♥ ♥ ♥

"When you pass through the waters, I will be with you; and when you pass through the rivers, they will not sweep over you."
Isaiah 43:2

I AM A
CHILD OF GOD

♥ ♥ ♥ ♥ ♥

"And I will be a
Father to you, and
you will be my sons
and daughters, says
the Lord Almighty."
2 Corinthians 6:18

I MEDITATE ON GOD's WORD

♥ ♥ ♥ ♥ ♥

"I have hidden your word in my heart, that I might not sin against You."

Psalm 119:11

I AM
BEAUTIFUL

♥ ♥ ♥ ♥ ♥

"You are altogether beautiful, my love; there is no flaw in you."
Song of Solomon 4:7

I AM
WISE

♥ ♥ ♥ ♥ ♥

"For through wisdom your days will be many, and years will be added to your life."
PROVERBS 9:11

I HAVE
PEACE

♥ ♥ ♥ ♥ ♥

"He makes me to lie down in green pastures; He leads me beside the still waters."
Psalm 23:2

GOD IS
WITH ME

"God is within her, she will not fall; God will help her at break of day."
Psalm 46:5

I AM
INQUISITIVE

♥ ♥ ♥ ♥ ♥

"Ask and it will be given to you; seek and you will find; knock and the door will be opened to you. For everyone who asks receives; the one who seeks finds; and to the one who knocks, the door will be opened."
Matthew 7:7-8

I CAN DO ANYTHING

"Don't let anyone look down on you because you are young, but set an example for the believers in speech, in conduct, in love, in faith and in purity."
1 Timothy 4:12

I AM GOD'S DAUGHTER

♥ ♥ ♥ ♥ ♥

"Know that the Lord is God; it is He who made us, and we are His; We are His people, and the sheep of His pasture." Psalm 100:3

I AM
DETERMINED

♥ ♥ ♥ ♥ ♥

"You will seek me and find me when you search for me with all your heart."
Jeremiah 29:13

I AM
SAFE

♥ ♥ ♥ ♥ ♥

"In peace I will lie down and sleep, for you alone, Lord, make me dwell in safety."
Psalm 4:8

I AM
SECURE

"If I take the wings of the morning and dwell in the uttermost parts of the sea, even there your hand shall lead me, and your right hand shall hold me."
Psalm 139:9

I CAN DO THIS

♥ ♥ ♥ ♥ ♥

"With God all things are possible."
Matthew 19:26

I AM AN HEIR

♥ ♥ ♥ ♥ ♥

"So you are no longer a slave, but God's child; and since you are his child, God has made you also an heir."
Galatians 4:7

WHO GOD SAYS I AM JOURNAL

YOU ARE
GOD'S
MASTERPIECE

RANDOM THOUGHTS

_____

_____

_____

ALL ABOUT ME

This is a picture of me ↷

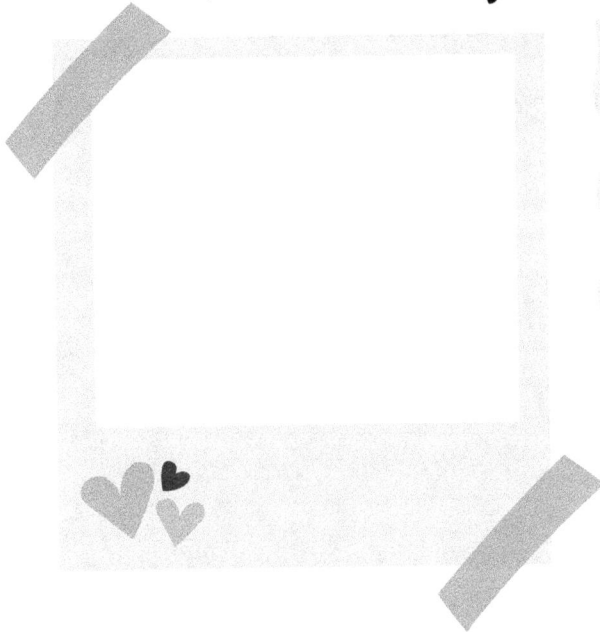

My name is

_____

_ _ _ _ _ _ _ _ _ _ _ _ _

_____

When I grow up, I want
to be a/an

_____

_ _ _ _ _ _ _ _ _ _ _ _ _

_____

_____

I am _____ years old.

This year, I want to learn more about

1 _____

_____

2 _____

_____

3 _____

_____

Write five (5) positive
descriptions about yourself, and
one (1) thing you can do or be.

I AM _____

I AM _____

I AM _____

I AM _____

I AM _____

I AM _____

I CAN _____

_____

GOD SAYS I AM

_____

JOURNALING PAGE

_____

_____

_____

_____

_____

_____

_____

_____

_____

_____

_____

_____

GOD SAYS I AM

_____

JOURNALING PAGE

GOD SAYS I AM

JOURNALING PAGE

GOD SAYS I AM

_____

JOURNALING PAGE

GOD SAYS I AM

_____

JOURNALING PAGE

_____

_____

_____

_____

_____

_____

_____

_____

_____

MY FAVORITE
BIBLE VERSE

MY NOTES

JOURNALING PAGE

_____

_____

_____

_____

_____

_____

_____

_____

_____

_____

_____

_____

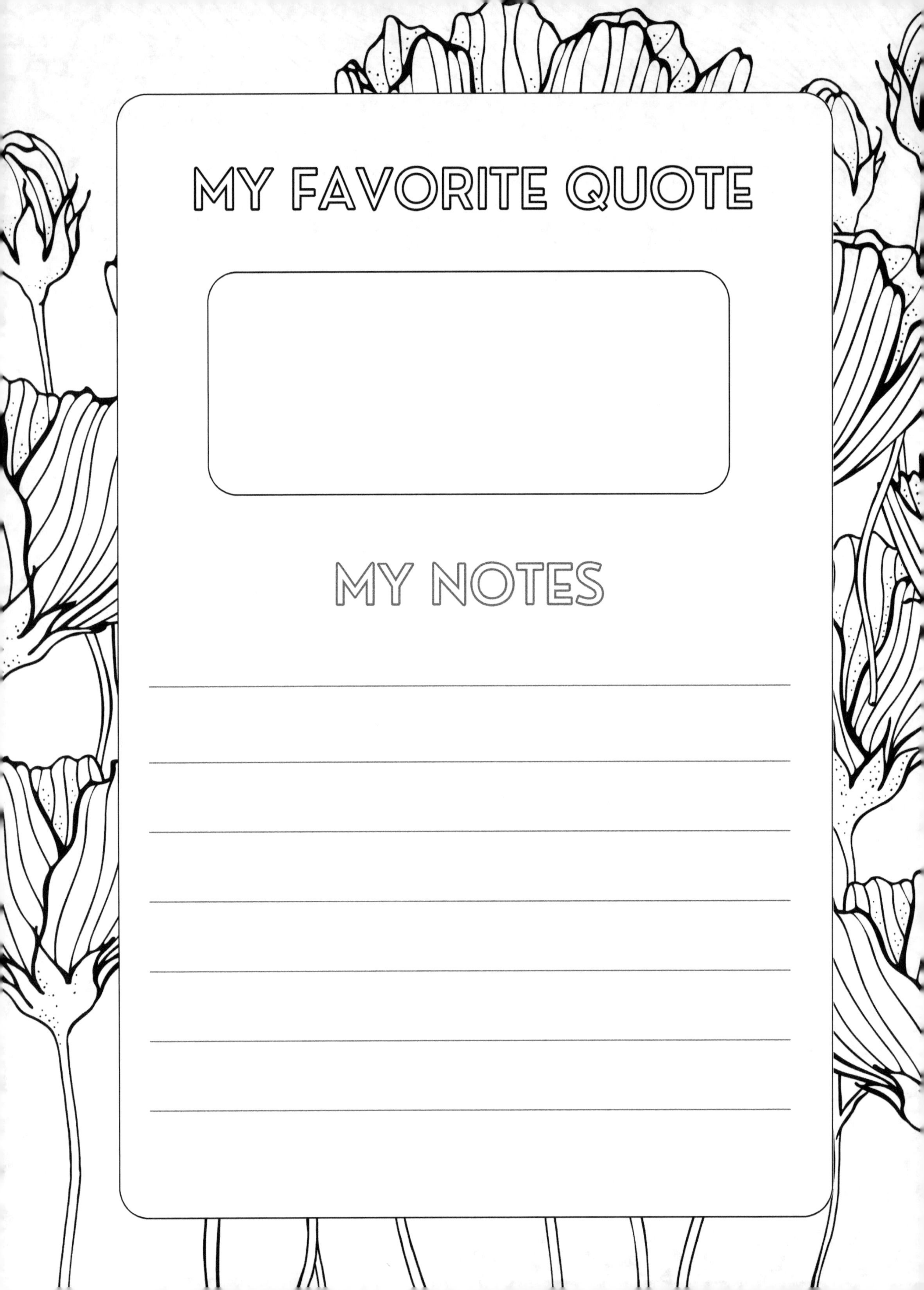

MY FAVORITE QUOTE

MY NOTES

JOURNALING PAGE

JOURNALING PAGE

MY FAVORITE JOKE

MY NOTES

JOURNALING PAGE

_____

_____

_____

_____

_____

_____

_____

_____

_____

_____

_____

JOURNALING PAGE

_____

_____

_____

_____

_____

_____

_____

_____

_____

_____

_____

GIVE THANKS

ALWAYS

I'M GRATEFUL FOR:

_____

_____

_____

_____

MY GOALS :

_____

_____

_____

_____

JOURNALING PAGE